Between Earth and Sky

poems by

Jo Kennedy

Finishing Line Press
Georgetown, Kentucky

Between Earth and Sky

Copyright © 2022 by Jo Kennedy
ISBN 978-1-64662-907-7 First Edition
All rights reserved under International and Pan-American Copyright Conventions. No part of this book may be reproduced in any manner whatsoever without written permission from the publisher, except in the case of brief quotations embodied in critical articles and reviews.

ACKNOWLEDGMENTS

My thanks to the following journals and their editors for publishing the following poems:

LINGERING IN THE MARGINS: Fire in the Bitterroots
PIEDMONT REVIEW: There Is No Death, Only a Change of Worlds
STREETLIGHT MAGAZINE: Swimming in Akumal, Still Life, Equinox
STREETLIGHT MAGAZINE 2017 ANTHOLOGY: Still Life, Equinox

The following poem in this collection also appeared in the chapbook *Wind River Song*, winner of the 1997 Anabiosis Chapbook Contest: There is No Death, Only a Change of Worlds.

Publisher: Leah Huete de Maines
Editor: Christen Kincaid
Cover Art: Jo Kennedy, *Can't See the Forest for the Trees*
Author Photo: Scott Elmquist
Cover Design: Elizabeth Maines McCleavy

Order online: www.finishinglinepress.com
also available on amazon.com

Author inquiries and mail orders:
Finishing Line Press
PO Box 1626
Georgetown, Kentucky 40324
USA

Table of Contents

Still Life 1

Between Earth and Sky 2

Shenandoah 4

Caretakers 6

Fire in the Bitterroots 7

Swimming in Akumal 8

Equinox 9

The Lockkeeper 10

Eden 11

Infestation 12

The Gift 13

Geography 14

Abacus 16

There Is No Death, Only a Change of Worlds 17

The Summer of Our Isolation 18

STILL LIFE

In the painting *Ram's Head with Hollyhock*,
there is a melding of bones and sky
and desert, no beginning or end,
just the eye sockets of a skull
transfixed on the faraway
and in the foreground, red hills and cedar.
I imagine O'Keefe walking in the desert
at night, catching a glint
at her feet—a shell, a stone—
and stooping to gather it up,
discovering the bleached bones
of a skull, vast and empty and beautiful,
like her desert. She must have rotated it
in her hands that night under the moon
as if it were a small earth, seeing in
its bony crevasses and arched jawline
the curvature of her own world,
its hills and arroyos alive in this skeleton
of animal. She must have heard the
echo of mountains, the rhythm of sky
in the labyrinth of bone.
And when she painted the yellow hollyhock
beside the skull, she must have seen
its petals ignite in flame,
a heart laid open
at its center, forever pressed
into bloom, into memory
of what we lose in the world,
then find again in hill and bone and sky.

BETWEEN EARTH AND SKY

Hang on tight, we're coming in—
your words
when the car spun out of control.
You said it as if
we were returning
home from a journey
to find just this world,
here on this night,
its own quiet beauty
after the storm,
a white space between earth and sky
where even the ice
is lovely in its treachery,
where a mountain road climbs
through pines and silver birch,
their branches frozen
against sky and two winter stars.

Even your voice is a surprise
in this stillness, your words
convincing us there is something
in the white calm
we can believe in,
hold onto, even love.

In a field nearby
deer are wandering,
grazing under the moon,
leaving their tracks in the snow.
In the morning they will return
to the familiar woods,
its circle of oak, juniper,
rhododendron draped in white.

They will come in from the world,
only to find it again
in this place between earth and sky,
its arbor of love,
rising and perennial.

SHENANDOAH

You've come home to care for our father,
this time to stay the winter. Mornings,
you wheel him along the riverbank,
watch the blue herons swoop

over cottonwoods and wade
in the shoals for fish. You listen
while he tells again the story
of the Indian chief who, watching
the river twist and swirl through the valley,
named it Shenandoah, Daughter of the Stars.
Nights, you read to him
from his favorite books, your letters
still pressed between earmarked pages.

You left the summer we got the Appaloosa.
I remember watching you kick your heels
into his belly as you rode bareback
and unbridled along the banks.
Later that summer, when the sun
scorched the valley cornfields brown,
you rode away and didn't return, this time
riding double on a Harley-Davidson, your arms
stretched around a light-haired boy,
his guitar strapped to your back like a papoose.

That winter we read your letters
mailed from a flat in Berkeley.
I wanted you home and waited for your return.
But when you didn't come,
I imagined you sitting
on a bare floor in your white jeans,
a string of turquoise around your neck,
your hair falling across your back.

Tonight, our fingers curved around steaming
mugs of tea, we sit and talk.
Years and distance have come between us.
We listen to the rasping breath
of our father in the next room.
The water ripples through its loamy riverbed.

CARETAKERS

We were young for such a holy office.
Sister shadows in the night,
we shimmied down the rain spout,
slipped through neighboring field
to the churchyard cemetery
where we plotted our territory,

staking claim
to this corner or that,
whichever needed tending most.
Kneeling down on the red clay,
we rubbed the soft cotton of our nightgowns
across the marble surfaces,
polishing each headstone
until it gleamed like the buffed
brass atop the church altar.

Tracing the letters with my fingertips,
I read aloud the names to you,
as if deciphering some ancient code
and because you wanted to know more
than names and dates, I told you stories
I could not have known.

Stories of blue babies and scarlet fever,
of accidental falls from silos,
of tractors overturning and corn threshers
mutilating, tales of daredevil dives
into the muddy north fork.

For even then we knew each life
had a story, each death's sorrow clear,
sweet as the summer night.

FIRE IN THE BITTERROOTS

At midnight
after the smoke had drifted
into the valley, we could see
the mountainside erupting in patches
of orange plume,
claiming hemlock, spruce,
cedar and pine.

In the summer drought
everything is on the verge of extinction,
even the garden of perennials we stand in,
one foot planted squarely in a bed
of lavender and lupine, the other
transfixed in its dream of the body
becoming a flame.

Just last summer we hiked the Bitterroots,
transfixed by their beauty
and calm—rocks, snowfields, alpine
wildflowers poking out
from clumps of earth, hungry
for light and air and sky.

Even then
at times we could almost feel
the tremor stirring beneath the earth,
could almost feel that place
smoldering beneath the rock.

Even then
we imagined we could hear
the taproot of life's desire,
beckoning us on,
calling us back.

SWIMMING IN AKUMAL

You could learn to live here
without ever measuring time
in linear seconds or distance
in the miles we journey.
Everything here is cyclical
and circular like the half moon
bay we swim in. Sun
and wind are nature's runes,
marking summer solstice, or storms
churning in from sea.

You could learn to forget here,
drifting in emerald water
among sea turtles and fish
the color of fruit—kiwi, mango, papaya—
and all around you, coral reefs rising
like sacred temples from the ocean's floor,
their exotic bloom luring
you beyond the cove,
tugging you to unfamiliar channels
of amnesia, uncharted dreams.

You could learn what it means
to love here, the red hibiscus
unfolding its petals to morning,
a beauty and clarity
as resonant as the tide.
At night you could taste the salt
on your lover's lips, knowing
you are tasting the earth,
knowing what it means
to love the world
we are adrift in.

EQUINOX

You spoke a language
we could not understand
just before you died, your last words
a gust of misplaced syllables
and I imagined you traveling
in another land, somewhere
between the continents of living
and dying, an equinox
where dark presses
against light, moon
against sun, where sky
and earth and even the trees
speak a foreign tongue. Sometimes
in the middle of the night,
awakened by a dream,
I stalk the house
in search of something
familiar and alive I can touch,
listen to. I play the piano,
stroke its keys,
water the amaryllis, planted
in stones as if in these hours
before daybreak I can awaken something
but even your photograph
is a still life, a fixture
in a world we are traveling
away from.

THE LOCKKEEPER

You write to tell me of a terrarium you found
buried in the hillside behind your house.
Inside a discarded bottle, a solitary world,
moss, wood fern and lichen, clinging
to stone and earth, stubborn
in its desire to live.

Living here in this stone house,
far away from anything,
you keep your own vigil
over countryside and canal,
its intricate litany of locks and gates.
After fifty years of living
you say you have nothing left to lose.

Is that why you've come here to this place
where at midnight you sit on a rock
in the middle of a field waiting
for the moon to dip behind the trees
or rise early to scour the morning sky
in search of a single red-tailed hawk?
Here, where you know the bluebirds will return in spring,
the periwinkle will leave its trail of purple
over the spring house roof,
here where the heart makes
its own nest against the storm?

EDEN

You would have done the same thing
had you been there in the garden,
so much beauty for the taking.
Sweet oleander and pink lehua,
eucalyptus and yellow ginger
calling your name in the night.

You too would have been drunk
on the spoils of fruit, if not apple,
plump ripe papaya, golden guava
or passion fruit dangling
from trees like small yellow moons.

It would have been impossible to imagine
the barrenness beyond the gate,
the river of loss flowing through craters.
Impossible, awaking as she did each morning
to birdsong and rainforests,
skies pink with promise.

And, yes, you too
would have made garlands
from the petals of the plumeria,
the very flower
that would be named
for the graves it adorned.

INFESTATION

Even the lentil stew, with its basil
and rosemary perfuming the steaming pot,
tasted like moths. For months
they permeated our lives,
blackening the white walls
where we splattered them,
infesting the corners of rooms,
inhabiting our dreams.
Aerosol sprays, swishing brooms,
slapping hands, large white
mothballs rolling from every shelf
like deadly marbles—nothing worked.
They were relentless.
They returned like old injuries,
bad habits we couldn't kick.
Lambswool, Shetland, cashmere, angora—
they knew no bounds.
Even my black silk gown
turned up, trailing a powdery web
of larva, waiting to spread its wings.
Not until we gave up,
admitted our consummate defeat,
did we discover the nesting place,
an old cupboard, hidden Indian corn,
its kernels pitted and infested.
That's the night I set fire
to the house, stood guard
on a nearby hill to watch it burn.

THE GIFT

I longed for the high-pitched song
of metal chimes, clinking
their sweet, ripe melody of summer night—
the kind that if you listen to long enough
you imagine you hear
a single white camellia
in your garden
opening its bloom to the dark
calling you to a moonlit field.

Instead you brought me chimes
made of coconut shells
and bamboo reeds
you bartered for in a tourist town.
You hung them from a limb
on the dogwood tree
where at night, bedroom window open,
I could hear their hollow
heavy bumping in the breeze,
their raspy breathing
invoking the thick chorus of night—
the clamor of tree frogs,
a back porch screen door
opening and closing with the wind,
an insistent siren pushing against time,
down the street a lost dog
wandering from house to house.
I asked for the wind song
of night dreams.
You brought me
The cacophony of life.

GEOGRAPHY

Each morning you brush your hair
and dress your Sunday best.
All dolled up for the day
of sitting in your chair
your eyes staring out
from someone else's face.
You touch the bracelet on your wrist
and count each green stone,
each gold link
as if to mark your days
on this strange abacus of time.

Lost in your own geography,
a world of uncharted continents
unmarked boundaries,
where oceans and rivers,
earth and sky scatter
into bedrock of memory and dream,
where sun no longer defines day,
nor moon, the night.
You imagine streams
are changing directions,
birds, flying in circles.
You have lost your bearing,
no compass can point you home.
Take my hand. Take me home.

Once, years ago
I let go of your hand,
wandering off in a crowded store.
I hid among dresses and shoe racks,
pretending a world of dress-up and glitter,
until I heard your voice calling
my name. Even then I recognized
the sound of loss
its fragile cadence of fear
thinning the air,
as if one syllable could tumble
the earth from its axis,
could pull a child from its mother
for a second, for eternity.

This time it is you who are wandering off,
your hand slipping away
from my fragile hold. This time,
a child, calling her mother back.
But I have no words you will know,
no name you will discern your own,
no language for this new country
you call home.
Take my hand. Take me home.

ABACUS

The closer you came to death,
the more alive your palette became.
Lavenders of evening sky
deepened to purple,
sunrise pinks bloomed crimson.
You blazed color across canvas
as if your brushstrokes could push away
the dark, could press into memory
the lake's shimmer, the leaf's
turning, the cardinal eating seed
on your windowsill.

You filled your canvases with images
you could no longer call
by name, words
you could not bring to mind.
Perhaps there is no language
for such loss.

I recall the day you composed
a list of seven subjects
you needed to discuss before the end.
I remember thinking of that list
as an abacus, each subject
a different color bead
on its spindle,
to be counted,
measured out against the hours.

THERE IS NO DEATH, ONLY A CHANGE OF WORLDS
Chief Seattle, Suquamish and Duwamish

I lie down in a bed of dry leaves,
feeling the crunch beneath me,
staring through the tops of cottonwood and aspen
until I'm sliding into sky,
falling into my father's words
the land ... it's all we can know.

Summer evenings, we'd ride the pickup truck
into the fields of tall grass to find them.
The smell of clover and honeysuckle
drifted through the windows like song.
We'd come upon them suddenly,
mother cow and her calf, bedded down,
its small body curved to hers,
still wet from its journey, wet
from the mother's tongue
licking it clean.

This is the way it should be then.
Body pressed to earth, trees sliding
to sky, not here in this room,
where white walls clot around you,
the ceiling hovering above you.
The stale breath of unwanted relatives.
Not here where your head
is propped on pillows,
your feet tucked and cornered
in the forced smile of sheets
starched white and stiff.
Here where you can only dream
of rising up and walking
through fields seeded with crops,
can only imagine turning the soil
in your fingers, its dark smell:
the land ... it's all we can know
still rich with its broken promise.

THE SUMMER OF OUR ISOLATION

Because you could not choose
otherwise, you left this earth
in the summer of our isolation
the long months of staring
through windows and doors
our faces shrouded in masks
our words muffled in fear.

You left when the purple hydrangea,
its underbelly of lush dreams,
had lost all hope of surviving
the long hot swelter of July,
the sycamore, its proud glory
bending low beneath the squat sun.

How have we come
to this neglect,
to this season of awful yearning?

Like the surprise of birdsong in early morning
you startled open the garden gate
and wandered out
leaving us in a daze of loss
a fever pitch of why?

As if tethered
we trailed behind you.
But you pointed us back,
back to the periphery of living
back to embrace
the terrible beauty of the earth
the fierceness of love.

Lean into loss, you said.
Lie down on its riverbank
and barter hard for life—

its reckless longing
its broken vows
its one constant
we can know, surrender to—

the sun rising in the east
evening unfolding to moonrise
stars scattering to dawn
the rapture
of it all. *Lean in
lean in.*

Jo Kennedy is a poet and painter living in Richmond, Virginia. Growing up in the Shenandoah Valley of Virginia, she spent much of her childhood in the out-of-doors, exploring fields and orchards, climbing trees and playing imaginary games with her sisters. Her interest in writing began in high school when she served as editor of her high school newspaper. She majored in English at Radford University and received a BS in English Education from Virginia Commonwealth University. She holds a Master of Humanities from the University of Richmond and a Master of Fine Arts in Poetry from Virginia Commonwealth University. While working on her first graduate degree, she completed course work in English literature at Cambridge University.

Jo taught composition, literature and creative writing at Virginia Commonwealth University, University of Richmond and Randolph-Macon College. She worked in communications in the corporate world for fourteen years before becoming the Director of the Visual Arts Center of Richmond where she established a creative writing program.

Jo's first chapbook *Wind River Song* was the 1997 winner of the Anabiosis Press Chapbook Contest. Her poems have been published in *Hawaii Pacific Review, Streetlight Magazine, Streetlight Magazine 2017 Anthology, Lingering in the Margins: River City Poets Anthology, Kansas Quarterly. Georgia State University Review, Cream City Review, Richmond Quarterly, California Quarterly, Oregon East, New Virginia Review, Florida Review* and other publications.

www.ingramcontent.com/pod-product-compliance
Lightning Source LLC
LaVergne TN
LVHW041525070426
835507LV00013B/1824